I0185457

Darkness Called Us Home

poems by

Rosemarie Wurth-Grice

Finishing Line Press
Georgetown, Kentucky

Darkness Called Us Home

Copyright © 2025 by Rosemarie Wurth-Grice
ISBN 979-8-88838-989-8 First Edition
All rights reserved under International and Pan-American Copyright Conventions.
No part of this book may be reproduced in any manner whatsoever without written
permission from the publisher, except in the case of brief quotations embodied in
critical articles and reviews.

ACKNOWLEDGMENTS

"On Returning Home" appeared in *Kentucky Monthly*
 "Hibernation" appeared in *Kudzu*

I'm grateful to these publications and to my family, friends, and fellow
writers of the Not Dead Poets' Society (NDPS) for their support through the
writing process.

Publisher: Leah Huete de Maines
Editor: Christen Kincaid
Cover Art and Design: Jonathon Wurth
Author Photo: Brittany Nichole Bunnell

Order online: www.finishinglinepress.com
             also available on amazon.com

Author inquiries and mail orders:
Finishing Line Press
PO Box 1626
Georgetown, Kentucky 40324
USA

Contents

To my family and friends
who have supported this writing journey

On Returning Home

What can I tell you?
The Scottish landscape changes
with the rain and sun and mist
Clouds gather
 in white and grey melancholy moods

filling the taller than this Kentucky sky

The names of villages
are not easy on the tongue
like the landscape, vowels and consonants
wind through mist and merge
in unfamiliar realms

On the River Clyde, gulls cackle
like crones drunk on too much ale
"A pint is never enough!" one shouts
and cackles again while grey feathers
float to the cobblestone below.

Come, sit with me by the window

We'll watch the rabbits fat and round,
gather on the old Abbey grounds
and wander into the monk's graveyard
to quietly nibble the velvet green moss
on Brother Ignatius' grave

Beyond the graves

The waters of Loch Ness are cold and black
stained from rain-washed peat
rolling off mountains separated an ice age ago
Both Scottish Highlands and Appalachians
exist here in slip fault fashion

and genetic memory swims deep

A Morning Note to John

Emily Dickinson wrote Remorse—is Memory—Awake
at window—and at Door

As I sit here at my kitchen table
sipping black coffee from a blue willow cup

The same cup I bought with savings stamps
when you were a child

The dog at my feet nibbles on crumbs
fallen from a blueberry muffin

I wish you could see from my window, John,
how the sun has splashed itself on the hillside

Two hawks have perched in the yellow poplar
searching for a breakfast of rabbit or squirrel

In shadow and sunlight
I've watched squirrels take great leaps of faith

Without thought of gravity or remorse
I took a leap once and carried you all with me

Notes from Teaching the Iliad and the Myth of Helen's Birth

So in this myth, I told the class
Zeus had a wandering eye
It wandered from mortal to mortal until
he spied Leda,
beautiful Leda, bride of Tyndareus
Leda, who had a fondness for swans

Imagine, I said, leaning in for effect—
the splendor and the horror
when he came to her that day—
a god in feathers

Yeats knew

And nine months later?
Some say the children hatched from two eggs
From one—Castor and Clytamnestra
From the other—Pollux and Helen, beautiful Helen
She knew how to launch a ship or two

Were they half swan? the bug-eyed, jaw-dropped teen
who always sat in the back row asked.

You must suspend your disbelief, I said
swatting white feathers out of the room

Of Madness and Morning Meditations

I

On days the madness creeps in
and I feel like a kite tethered to the ground by a silver thread
floating on a current of lavender spiced air
being tugged and pulled through gusts and gales
this little piece of earth is where the silver thread holds me

II

On these days of morning madness
I sometimes think of Kipling and his son
the boy he pushed to be a soldier, who went to war
and was lost, never to be found.
I think of guilt and honor, pride and regret
of how difficult finding one's place in the world can be
of how easy it is to be lost

III

When my soldier son called home
his voice traveling across a thousand miles of prairie dust,
wagon ruts, red rock, and blue stem grass
to these rolling hills and winding roads
to a place where the distance somehow brought us closer
I wished then I could take away the loneliness that youth and the
strangeness of growing up far from home can bring.
How odd that just the sound of a voice
familiar as breath can save us

IV

And now time has stretched the years so thin
that light shines through
We stare into the luminous darkness of *What ifs*
black and glossy as the raven's wing
looking for ourselves
How easy it is to be lost

One for Sorrow

a written response to "Soiree" a painting by Andrea Kowch
and the nursery rhyme "One for Sorrow"

I'm not as I once was, yet still lost
Trying to find my way through this forest
wandering amidst trees that continue to fall
The dead stand on hope
the dying drop one brown leaf at a time

An artist, not I, dreamt up this sordid soiree
a girl on a hill sits among avian oracles
an October wind rips pages from her hymnal
Blessed Assurance disappears in a grief grey sky

Does she count two for joy or three for a girl
discover seven for secrets untold
until fourteen crows sport on the canvas
one more than the devil himself?

Will the crows come to tea if I spread a blanket,
put out cookies, sweet fruit, and fresh baked pie?
Will they drink thick cream, and herbal tea from fine china?

I wonder what happens
if I step out of this picture
left the girl with her choices and frolicking crows
Would being free and being lost feel the same?

Rabbit Holes

Lately

my thoughts   stray to places

I've long   since left

They hop   and multiply

until the room is filled with white rabbits
each shouting
there is no time to say hello,
goodbye,
then rush out the door
into the garden
to become
brown hares frolicking in the blackberry bushes

I sit here with the small silences when they leave
until the ringing in my head drowns out the quiet
a constant reminder of the past's loud noises

Thunder rolls in from the west
Rain pours through the hole in the roof
The rabbits fill up the room again

Ninety-five Moons of Jupiter

I am lost for words
        a bat flying at night
                mouth wide open
                        singing echo, echo, echo

Metaphors collide
        meanings hide like chameleons in a tapestry of flowers
                Cosmos, amaranth, and celosia are my
earthbound galaxies

A moonflower unfurls at dusk and reaches toward Jupiter
        and there I am—one moon of ninety-five
                Ganymeade, orbiting once
                        while Europa passes by twice

And Io? She circles four times
        in resonance, they say
                Yet nothing resonates on the page
                        as I plod along in orbital eccentricity

An ellipses of planetary motion,
        I try to make some logic of this scientific magic,
                I put despair and hope in a bottle and cast names
to the stars
                With mouth wide open,

I croak an echolocation from the heart

Sunday Morning Self-Realization

—discovered on half a dozen legal pads scattered about
and a poem the dog chewed on but found unpalatable

I
Odin traveled the nine worlds and spoke only in poems
I walked across the pasture and wrote a list of grief-bent
metaphors

II
In my other life
I couldn't swim and sailed the Titanic
My mother named me Constance
I could sing

III
I scribbled titles of books I'll never write
like *Flying Pigs and other Airborne Livestock,*
Black Patent Leather Shoes and Other Atrocities

IV
My mother, nearly deaf, sometimes hears music
and a Pentecostal preacher outside her bedroom
My husband, in the hospital, chatted with his dead brother
Who will I hear?

V
The dog chewed on this:
I am a widow
A woman who has outlived the man to whom she was
married.
Deprived of something valued, bereaved
In printing, an incomplete line, as that ending a paragraph,
carried
*over to the top of a new page**

In my case, a legal pad

Vestigial

—forming a very small remnant of something that was once larger

You gave me memories I could have tucked away
like cherished linens in a cedar-lined chest

but you knew I could never fold anything neatly.

Instead, these memories are glistening salamanders with
vestigial tails—old survivors of life's skirmishes.

They swim beneath the surface of woodland streams
where light glides gently over the cedars

as effortless as birds in flight

An October Pantoum of Sorts

On this hill of loneliness, a solitary bee is sleeping
curled upon a flower stalk beneath a star mad sky
Shall we sing to the hive tonight *Your keeper has died?*
Hold your breath awhile, for it's breathing that gives us away

Curled upon a flower stalk beneath a star mad sky
can we weigh the universe in the cup of our hands?
Hold your breath awhile, for it's breathing that gives us away
Listen to the tremble of a million leaves

Can we weigh the universe in the cup of our hands?
The Earth whisperer is a forest of a single dying tree
Listen to the tremble of a million leaves
Comet dust illuminating the birthing of a world

The Earth whisperer is a forest of a single dying tree
a lone quaking aspen, Pando in Latin, *I spread*
comet dust. Illuminating the birthing of a world
on this hill of loneliness, a solitary bee is sleeping

Winter Rain

Listen to the sky shedding
wet shades of grey

a thousand cat feet
tromping on the eaves

To sit here by a fire
solitary

except
for a small sleeping dog

is to be content in warm
sylvan silences

Seasons Mean Nothing

Now that I'm old, my head is full with the humming of cicadas
those constant companions regardless the season

Now while I sit in the shadow of a great swaying mimosa
that fell in a storm when I was fifteen

Now while I walk through summer's blackberry brambles
your horses gallop past me in the fresh fallen snow

Now that they've gone, father, brother, and lover
I listen for their voices
In grief, they say, voices are the first to go

The cicadas keep filling my head with phantom summers
The mimosa has not grown back but continues to sway

The horses are gone but still run in the pasture
I read your poem just yesterday.

How is it Possible?

In Memoriam for Keaton & Ford

How is it possible?
You left and the sun still rose
Children stirred from their slumber
Birds gathered in hedges and sang

You left and we fell silent
expecting you to fill the doorway
take a seat at our table

You left and the room echoes
with your emptiness

How is it possible?
With your last breath,
we kept breathing

Hibernation

On the anniversary of my brother's death

It's time to go into my cave again
The dry leaves in the forest hum a lullaby
The dusk foretells an early frost

I've gorged on trout and pomegranate
My walk grows slow and padded
clawed tree bark marks my trail

Soon there will be winter dreams of ripe
raspberries and cold streams to wash my face

What are twenty years to us my brother?
I thought of you in the last days…you on your
mountaintop looking over the world

One day you fell asleep and forgot to wake

I'll sweep the cave floor clean of bones
and lay down to sleep the old sleep
among pine boughs and moss
owl feathers and rabbit fur

If there are dreams in death
look for me on the mountain trail
ambling along the timberline

Shadow Dreams

My dreams and I have grown apart
—Alexander Pushkin

You have a place but your place is not here
gone long ago a shade that returns in December
walks past me through the ashes of a phoenix
taking flight across the pasture

a shadow in a wrinkled shirt now pressed
mud-caked boots polished
the scent of cedar and fresh mown hay lost
in the soft warmth of your flesh gone

You have a place but your place is not here

Shindy Coats and Pagan Fires

After W.B. Yeats

I
I made my song a shindy *coat*
wore its sum and substance against the gales
of boredom and good intentions
Kept shivers from the bone with woolen lyrics
that felt thick on the tongue after nights of too much
wine and wonderlust

II
I might be a mud-brained ballad-monger
gone mad sailing down rivulets of rhyme
thumbing through silver-fished volumes
thunderstruck by Oliver or Yeats
Shall I attend a tea party for the dead
or find peace with poets in owl-light and red wine?

III
But wait! It's the beginning of the end
of winter - Imbolc, St. Brigid's Day
Love fled and paced upon the mountain
while nuns kept the fires going for 500 years
stoking their faith upon faith and the memory of pagan fires

IV
Come, drink milk from a sacred cow
Light your fire from the flame that burned in Brigid's head
 Burn baby burn! Wail for the dead of winter!
Shout three Hail Mary's and please, change the milk to wine

Illustration by Jonathon Wurth

Born in small town Elkton, Kentucky, **Rosemarie Wurth-Grice** grew up reading and writing poetry. She graduated with a B.A. in Journalism and a M.A. in English and Creative Writing from Western Kentucky University in Bowling Green.

She is a retired High School English and AP Language and Composition teacher and founding member of the Not Dead Poets' Society (NDPS), a writing group which meets regularly to provide support to local poets and writers.

Her poetry and/or short stories have appeared in *Kentucky Monthly, Kudzu, Kentucky English Bulletin,* and the *Journal of Kentucky Studies.*

A widow and mother of three grown sons, the poet lives on her cut flower and blackberry farm near the banks of the Barren River. Here, she wrote her chapbook *Darkness Called Us Home,* a reflective anthology of poems that delve into a life spent raising sons, teaching English, tending her flowers, knowing great love, and suffering great loss. Her poetry examines the personal and universal human condition through the lens of the natural landscape, a landscape that is the setting of her past, present, and future where all three timelines overlap in memories. grief, and finding healing in poetry and the natural world.

www.ingramcontent.com/pod-product-compliance
Lightning Source LLC
Chambersburg PA
CBHW030053100426
42734CB00038B/1538